America's GREAT WILDERNESS

in the words of **Henry David Thoreau**
John Muir
John Burroughs
Theodore Roosevelt
Stewart L. Udall

David Sumner

The rugged Salmon River, Idaho.

Home Library Publishing Company
Fort Atkinson, Wisconsin

Texas Parks and Wildlife Dept.

The lush banks of the Brazos River, central Texas.

Excerpt from *An Autobiography* by Theodore Roosevelt copyright 1913 by Charles Scribner's Sons, renewal copyright 1941 by Edith K. Carow Roosevelt; reprinted with permission of Charles Scribner's Sons.

CONTENTS

Introduction **4**

  I **The Phenomena of Nature**
Henry David Thoreau **6**

 II **In the Western Wilderness**
John Muir **22**

III **Wilds Along the Hudson**
John Burroughs **50**

IV **The Conservationist President**
Theodore Roosevelt **70**

 V **America's Parklands at the Crossroads**
Stewart L. Udall **82**

INTRODUCTION

Just over four hundred years ago, America was an unknown wilderness, full of vast forests, clear streams and lakes, unspoiled deserts and grasslands. But European settlers saw the wilderness as something to overcome, and since then the idea has been slow to die. Today, Americans are finally awakening to the need of preserving what is left of their great wilderness. Much of the credit for this realization lies with Henry David Thoreau, John Muir, John Burroughs, Theodore Roosevelt, and modern conservationists such as Stewart L. Udall.

There can be little doubt that the past century has brought us to a greater understanding and appreciation of the thoughts, attitudes and vision of Henry David Thoreau, naturalist, essayist, social critic, poet.

Thoreau's concern for bringing man into harmony with his environment speaks directly to today's environmental problems. While rambling through the fields near his beloved Concord, Massachusetts, Thoreau seems to have probed the soul of modern man with a deliberation and insight few men since can equal.

Thoreau was born in Concord in 1817 of an intelligent family with few financial resources. In 1845 he built a cabin on some land owned by Ralph Waldo Emerson in the woods beside Walden Pond because, he later wrote, "I wished to live deliberately, to front only the essential facts of life, and see if I could learn what it had to teach." He lived there two years, removed from the village, but not as a hermit. He went into Concord almost every day and passersby visited him in his cabin from time to time.

Because he realized the need of man for the natural world, no other writer has treasured the gifts of the American land as did he.

John Muir's main influence as a conservationist came through his articles and books about his personal experiences in the wilds, especially in the Far West and Alaska. Throughout these narratives he wove his philosophy of wilderness values.

Born in 1838 in Scotland, young John and his family moved to the Wisconsin frontier where their pioneer life was a hard one. Contrary to the hostile attitude toward wilderness that hardship produced in their neighbors, Muir's father taught his children that nature showed forth the glory and power of God, thus allowing John to see beyond the normal frontier prejudices against wilderness.

In 1871, three years after his arrival in California, he published the first of his conservation articles, urging the protection of Yosemite. It was the beginning of a crusade that climaxed with the establishment of Yosemite National Park in 1890. To protect this and other legislative gains, he organized the Sierra Club in 1892.

Born in New York State in 1837, John Burroughs lived during a time when the North American continent was still relatively wild and undeveloped. While all parts of the Catskills and Adirondacks of New York State were home to him, it was Riverby, his farm on the banks of the mighty Hudson River, Slabsides, his hidden retreat, and his bark study at Riverby where he really belonged.

He met John Muir in Yosemite, was a personal friend of Theodore Roosevelt and many other eminent figures, but while he treasured these relationships, he felt more at home with the woodchucks, thrushes and warblers of his native woods and those who came to visit him there.

For him, wilderness did not necessarily mean unbroken reaches of wild country but could be found in a thicket of honeysuckle, a patch of tundra above timberline, or a little swamp fed by a spring. Through these gleanings from a lifetime of writing runs a golden thread, the thought that the key to fulfillment is being in tune with the cosmos and at one with every living thing.

Theodore Roosevelt once said that if he had not experienced the joy and adventure of ranch life in the Dakotas, he never would have become President. Roosevelt's attitude toward the environment made him our first conservationist President at a time when much political power was needed to begin preserving America's diminishing wilderness.

Born in New York City in 1858, "TR," although sickly as a boy, developed a great interest in natural history and athletics which led him to go west in 1883 to run a cattle ranch and hunt in North Dakota. Enduring the hard life of a cowboy, he nevertheless appreciated the wilderness environment of prairie grass, badlands and buffalo, which were at that time being slaughtered by the thousands by careless hunters. Although he was a hunter himself, he was not indiscriminate and saw beauty in all things.

As President, he was instrumental in establishing a great many of our national parks and in promoting our twentieth-century wilderness ethic.

Other conservationists have continued where Teddy Roosevelt left off, including Stewart L. Udall, Secretary of the Interior under Presidents Kennedy and Johnson. Udall's concern for the environment goes beyond simply establishing more parks and wilderness areas. He is also concerned with preserving our present parklands against commercialization, overlogging, chemical poisoning, air and water pollution, strip mining, and visitor overuse of our national parks.

These modern environmental ills have caused what Udall calls a conservation crisis, but, he adds, we have the ability to eliminate them, if we also have the desire.

Ed Cooper

Pines in the Sierra Nevada Mountains, California.

HENRY DAVID THOREAU

I The Phenomena of Nature

As I sat on the high bank at the east end of Walden, ...
I saw, by a peculiar intention or dividing of the eye, a very
striking subaqueous rainbow-like phenomenon.... Those
brilliant shrubs, which were from three to a dozen feet in
height, were all reflected, dimly so far as the details of
leaves, etc., were concerned, but brightly as to color, and,
of course, in the order in which they stood, — scarlet,
yellow, green, etc.; but, there being a slight ripple on the
surface, these reflections were not true to their height
though true to their breadth, but were extended
downward with mathematical perpendicularity, three or
four times too far, forming sharp pyramids of the several
colors, gradually reduced to mere dusky points. The effect
of this prolongation of the reflection was a very pleasing
softening and blending of the colors, especially when a
small bush of one bright tint stood directly before another
of a contrary and equally bright tint. It was just as if you
were to brush firmly aside with your hand or a brush a
fresh line of paint of various colors, or so many lumps of
friable colored powders.

Journal, October 7, 1857

Autumn colors, New Hampshire. Thoreau saw such
scenes daily, yet never tired of their beauty. He realized
that man needed his natural surroundings for survival.

7

Walden Pond near Concord, Massachusetts. Thoreau built his cabin at the pond because he wished to "live deliberately, to front only the essential facts of life. . . ."

Ed Cooper

8

A rare photograph of Thoreau at about age 30.

Another perfect Indian-summer day. Some small bushy white asters still survive.

The autumnal tints grow gradually darker and duller, but not less rich to my eye. And now a hillside near the river exhibits the darkest, crispy reds and browns of every hue, all agreeably blended. At the foot, next the meadow, stands a front rank of smoke-like maples bare of leaves, intermixed with yellow birches. Higher up, are red oaks of various shades of dull red, with yellowish, perhaps black oaks intermixed, and walnuts, now brown, and near the hilltop, or rising above the rest, perhaps, a still yellow oak, and here and there amid the rest or in the foreground on the meadow, dull ashy salmon-colored white oaks large and small, all these contrasting with the clear liquid, sempiternal green of pines.

Journal, October 25, 1852

It is wonderful what gradation and harmony there is in nature. The light reflected from bare twigs at this season ... is not only like that from gossamer, but like that which will ere long be reflected from the ice that will incrust them. So the bleached herbage of the field is like frost, and frost like snow, and one prepares for the other.

Journal, November 13, 1858

These are true mornings of creation, original and poetic days . . .

These are true mornings of creation, original and poetic days, not mere repetitions of the past. There is no lingering of yesterday's fogs, only such a mist as might have adorned the first morning.

Journal, January 6, 1858

Every part of nature teaches that the passing away of one life is the making room for another. The oak dies down to the ground, leaving within its rind a rich virgin mould, which will impart a vigorous life to an infant forest. The pine leaves a sandy and sterile soil, the harder woods a strong and fruitful mould.

So this constant abrasion and decay makes the soil of our future growth. As I live now so shall I reap. If I grow pines and birches, my virgin mould will not sustain the oak; but pines and birches, or, perchance, weeds and brambles, will constitute my second growth.

Journal, October 24, 1837

The landscape looked singularly clean and pure and dry, the air, like a pure glass, being laid over the picture, the trees so tidy, and stripped of their leaves; the meadows and pastures, clothed with clean dry grass, looked as if they had been swept; ice on the water and winter in the air; but yet not a particle of snow on the ground. The woods, divested in great part of their leaves, are being ventilated. It is the season of perfect works, of hard, tough, ripe twigs, not of tender buds and leaves. The leaves have made their wood, and a myriad new withes stand up all around pointing to the sky, able to survive the cold. It is only the perennial that you see, the iron age of the year.

Journal, November 25, 1850

For the first week, whenever I look out on the pond it impressed me like a tarn high up on the side of a mountain, its bottom far above the surface of other lakes, and, as the sun rose, I saw it throwing off its nightly clothing of mist, and here and there, by degrees, its soft ripples or its smooth reflecting surface was revealed, while the mists, like ghosts, were stealthily withdrawing in every direction into the woods, as at the breaking up of some nocturnal conventicle. The very dew seemed to hang upon the trees later into the day than usual, as on the sides of mountains.

Walden

G. C. Kelley

Above: Porcupine in late spring.
Opposite: Maple tree in autumn.

Rural river scene, New England.

*I want to go soon
and live away by the
pond, where I shall
hear only the wind . . .*

I was reminded, this morning before I rose, of those undescribed ambrosial mornings of summer which I can remember, when a thousand birds were heard gently twittering and ushering in the light, like the argument to a new canto of an epic and heroic poem. The serenity, the infinite promise, of such a morning! The song or twitter of birds drips from the leaves like dew. Then there was something divine and immortal in our life, when I have waked up on my couch in the woods and seen the day dawning, and heard the twittering of the birds.

Journal, March 10, 1852

And the water-lily floats on the smooth surface of slow waters, amid rounded shields of leaves, bucklers, red beneath, which stimulate a green field, perfuming the air. Each instantly the prey of the spoiler, — the rose-bug and water-insects. How transitory the perfect beauty of the rose and the lily! The highest, intensest color belongs to the land, the purest, perchance, to the water. The lily is perhaps the only flower which all are eager to pluck; it may be partly because of its inaccessibility to most.

Journal, June 26, 1852

This is June, the month of grass and leaves. The deciduous trees are investing the evergreens and revealing how dark they are. Already the aspens are trembling again, and a new summer is offered me. I feel as little fluttered in my thoughts, as if I might be too late. Each season is but an infinitesimal point. It no sooner comes than it is gone. It has no duration. It simply gives a tone and hue to my thought.

Each annual phenomenon is a reminiscence and prompting. Our thoughts and sentiments answer to the revolutions of the seasons, as two cog-wheels fit into each other. We are conversant with only one point of contact at a time, from which we receive a prompting and impulse and instantly pass to a new season or point of contact. A year is made up of a certain series and number of sensations and thoughts which have their language in nature. Now I am ice, now I am sorrel. Each experience reduces itself to a mood of the mind.

Journal, June 6, 1857

Within a little more than a fortnight the woods, from bare twigs, have become a sea of verdure, and young shoots have contended with one another in the race. The leaves are unfurled all over the country. . . . Shade is produced, and the birds are concealed and their economies go forward uninterruptedly, and a covert is afforded to animals generally. But thousands of worms and insects are preying on the leaves while they are young and tender. Myriads of little parasols are suddenly spread all the country over, to shield the earth and the roots of the trees from the parching heat, and they begin to flutter and rustle in the breeze. Checkerberry shoots . . . are now just fit to eat . . . .

Journal, June 1, 1854

I want to go soon and live away by the pond, where I shall hear only the wind whispering among the reeds. It will be success if I shall have left myself behind. But my friends ask what I will do when I get there. Will it not be employment enough to watch the progress of the seasons?

Journal, December 24, 1841

The wilderness is near, as well as dear, to every man. Even the oldest villages are indebted to the border of wild wood which surrounds them, more than to the gardens of men. There is something indescribably inspiriting and beautiful in the aspect of the forest skirting and occasionally jutting into the midst of new towns, which, like the sand-heaps of fresh fox burrows, have sprung up in their midst. The very uprightness of the pines and maples asserts the ancient rectitude and vigor of nature. Our lives need the relief of such a background, where the pine flourishes and the jay still screams.

A Week on the Concord and Merrimack Rivers

Morning fog on a pond. Thoreau found solitude such as this a subject for writing.

We dipped our way between fresh masses of foliage
overrun with grape and smaller flowering vines . . .

As we thus dipped our way along between fresh masses of foliage overrun with the grape and smaller flowering vines, the surface was so calm, and both air and water so transparent, that the flight of a kingfisher or robin over the river was as distinctly seen reflected in the water below as in the air above. The birds seemed to flit through submerged groves, alighting on the yielding sprays, and their clear notes to come up from below. We were uncertain whether the water floated the land, or the land held the water in its bosom. . . . For every oak and birch too growing on the hilltop, as well as for these elms and willows, we knew that there was a graceful, ethereal and ideal tree making down from the roots, and sometimes Nature in high tides brings her mirror to its foot and makes it visible. The stillness was intense and almost conscious, as if it were a natural Sabbath. The air was so elastic and crystalline that it had the same effect on the landscape that a glass has on a picture, to give it an ideal remoteness and perfection. The landscape was clothed in a mild and quiet light, in which the woods and fences checkered and partitioned it with new regularity, and rough and uneven fields stretched away with lawn-like smoothness to the horizon, and the clouds, finely distinct and picturesque, seemed a fit drapery to hang over fairy-land. The world seemed decked for some holyday or prouder pageantry, with silken streamers flying, and the course of our lives to wind on before us like a green lane into a country maze, at the season when fruit trees are in blossom.

Why should not our whole life and its scenery be actually thus fair and distinct? All our lives want a suitable background. . . . Character always secures for itself this advantage, and is thus distinct and unrelated to near or trivial objects whether things or persons.

A Week on the Concord and Merrimack Rivers

A small stream erodes its rocky bed into a miniature canyon.

Grant Heilman

As I come over the hill, I hear the wood thrush singing his evening lay. This is the only bird whose note affects me like music, affects the flow and tenor of my thoughts, my fancy and imagination. It lifts and exhilarates me. It is inspiring. It is a medicative draught to my soul. It is an elixir to my eyes and a fountain of youth to all my senses. It changes all hours to an eternal morning. It banishes all trivialness. It reinstates me in my dominion, makes me the lord of creation, is chief musician of my court. This minstrel sings in a time a heroic age, with which no event in the village can be contemporary. How can they be contemporary when only the latter is *temporary* at all? . . .So there is something in the music of the cow-bell, something sweeter and more nutritious, than in the milk which the farmers drink. This thrush's song is a *ranz des vaches* to me. I long for wildness, a nature which I cannot put my foot through, woods where the wood thrush forever sings, where the hours are early morning ones, and there is dew on the grass, and the day is forever unproved, where I might have a fertile unknown for a soil about me. I would go after the cows, I would watch the flocks of Admetus there forever, only for my board and clothes, a New Hampshire everlasting and unfallen . . . All that was ripest and fairest in the wildness and the wild man is preserved and transmitted to us in the strain of the wood thrush. It is the mediator between barbarism and civilization. It is unrepentant as Greece.

Journal, June 22, 1853

Each new year is a surpise to us. We find that we had virtually forgotten the note of each bird, and when we hear it again it is remembered like a dream, reminding us of a previous state of existence. How happens it that the associations it awakens are always pleasing, never saddening; reminiscences of our sanest hours? The voice of nature is always encouraging.

Journal, March 18, 1858

Strange that so few ever come to the woods to see how the pine lives and grows and spires, lifting its evergreen arms to the light, — to see its perfect success. . . .

The Maine Woods

Pines and sumac bushes along an Eastern river.

I went to the woods because I wished to live deliberately, to front only the essential facts of life, and see if I could not learn what it had to teach, and not, when I came to die, discover that I had not lived.

Walden

In this fresh evening each blade and leaf looks as if it had been dipped in an icy liquid greenness. Let eyes that ache come here and look . . . .

Journal, June 30, 1840

As the afternoons grow shorter, and the early evening drives us home to complete our chores, we are reminded of the shortness of life, and become more pensive. . . . I seemed to recognize the November evening as a familiar thing come round again. . . . It appeared like a part of a panorama at which I sat spectator, a part with which I was perfectly familiar just coming into view, and I foresaw how it would look, and prepared to be pleased. . . . What new sweet was I to extract from it?

. . . There is no more tempting novelty than this new November.

Journal, November 1, 1858

I am disturbed by the sound of my steps on the frozen ground. I wish to hear the silence of the night, for the silence is something positive and to be heard. I cannot walk with my ears covered. I must stand still and listen with open ears, far from the noises of the village, that the night may make its impression on me. A fertile and eloquent silence. Sometimes the silence is merely negative, an arid and barren waste in which I shudder, where no ambrosia grows. I must hear the whispering of a myriad voices. Silence alone is worthy to be heard. Silence is of various depths and fertility, like soil. Now it is a mere Sahara, where men perish of hunger and thirst, now a fertile bottom, or prairie, of the West. As I leave the village, drawing nearer to the woods, I listen from time to time to hear the hounds of Silence baying at the Moon, — to know if they are on the track of any game. If there's no Diana in the night, what is it worth? . . . The silence rings; it is musical and thrills me. A night in which the silence was audible. I heard the unspeakable.

Journal, January 21, 1853

The site of Thoreau's cabin
at Walden Pond, Massachusetts.

Charles R. Fowler

I wished to live deliberately, to front only the essential facts . . .

17

Nature is full of genius, full of divinity;
so that not a snowflake escapes its fashioning hand. . .

The thin snow now driving from the north and lodging on my coat consists of those beautiful star crystals, not cottony and chubby spokes, as on the 13th December, but thin and partly transparent crystals. . . . How full of the creative genius is the air in which these are generated! I should hardly admire more if real stars fell and lodged on my coat. Nature is full of genius, full of the divinity; so that not a snowflake escapes its fashioning hand. . . . The same law that shapes the earth-star shapes the snow-star. . . .

What a world we live in! where myriads of these little disks, so beautiful to the most prying eye, are whirled down on every traveler's coat, the observant and the unobservant, and on the restless squirrel's fur, and on the far-stretching fields and forests, the wooded dells, and the mountain-tops. Far, far away from the haunts of man, they roll down some little slope, fall over and come to their bearings, and melt or lose their beauty in the mass, ready anon to swell some little rill with their contribution, and so, at last, the universal ocean from which they came. There they lie, like the wreck of chariot-wheels after a battle in the skies.

Journal, January 5, 1856

Phil McCafferty

Above me the cloudless blue sky; beneath, the . . . sky-reflecting ice. . . At a distance in several directions I see the tawny earth streaked or spotted with white where the bank or hills and fields appear, or else the green-black evergreen forests, or the brown or russet, or tawny deciduous woods, and here and there, where the agitated surface of the river is exposed, the blue-black water. That dark-eyed water, especially where I see it at right angles with the direction of the sun, is it not the first sign of spring? How its darkness contrasts with the general lightness of the winter! It has more life in it than any part of the earth's surface. It is where one of the arteries of the earth is palpable, visible.

Journal, February 12, 1860

Left: Ice breaks up on an Eastern stream.
Opposite: A fresh snowfall covers evergreens.

In the brooks the slight grating sound of small cakes of ice, floating with various speed, is full of content and promise, and where the water gurgles under a natural bridge, you may hear these hasty rafts hold conversation in an undertone. Every rill is a channel for the juices of the meadow. Last year's grasses and flower-stalks have been steeped in rain and snow, and now the brooks flow with meadow tea, — thoroughwort, mint, flagroot, and pennyroyal, all at one draught.

Journal, March 8, 1840

I perceive the spring in the softened air. . . . Apparently in consequence of the very warm sun . . . falling on the earth four-fifths covered with snow and ice, there is an almost invisible vapor held in suspension. . . . Looking through this transparent vapor, all surfaces, not osiers and open water alone, look more vivid. The hardness of winter is relaxed.

There is a fine effluence surrounding the wood, as if the sap had begun to stir and you could detect it a mile off. Such is the difference between an object seen through a warm, moist, and soft air and a cold, dry, hard one. Such is the genialness of nature that the trees appear to have put out feelers by which the senses apprehend them more tenderly. I do not know that the woods are ever more beautiful, or affect me more.

Journal, March 10, 1859

Still cold and blustering. . . . How silent are the footsteps of spring! There, too, where there is a fraction of the meadow, two rods over, quite bare, under the bank, in this warm recess at the head of the meadow, though the rest of the meadow is covered with snow a foot or more depth, I am surprised to see the skunk-cabbage, with its great spear-heads open and ready to blossom. . . . The spring advances in spite of snow and ice, and cold even.

Journal, March 30, 1856

This is the first really spring day. . . . The sound of distant crows and cocks is full of spring. . . . Something analogous to the thawing of the ice seems to have taken place in the air. At the end of winter there is a season in which we are daily expecting spring, and finally a day when it arrives. . . .

Journal, March 10, 1853

Sunset colors are reflected from a rippled lake.

JOHN MUIR

II In the Western Wilderness

In the spring, after all the avalanches are down and the snow is melting fast, it is glorious to hear the streams sing out on the mountains.

Our National Parks

Climb the mountains and get their good tidings. Nature's peace will flow into you as the sunshine flows into trees. The winds will blow their own freshness into you, and the storms their energy, while cares will drip off like autumn leaves.

Our National Parks

Benevolent, solemn, fateful, pervaded with divine light, every landscape glows like a countenance hallowed in eternal repose; and every one of its living creatures, clad in flesh and leaves, and every crystal of its rocks, whether on the surface shining in the sun or buried miles deep in what we call darkness, is throbbing and pulsing with the heartbeats of God.

Our National Parks

Mount Morrison in California's Sierra Nevada Mountains. Muir loved the Sierras and pushed for their preservation, especially of Yosemite Valley and the giant sequoias.

Ed Cooper

Ed Cooper

There is always something deeply exciting, not only in the sounds of winds in the woods, which exert more or less influence over every mind, but in their varied water-like flow as manifested by the movements of the trees, especially those of the conifers. By no other trees are they rendered so extensively and impressively visible, not even by the lordly tropic palms or tree-ferns responsive to the gentlest breeze. The waving of a forest of the giant sequoias is indescribably impressive and sublime, but the pines seem to me the best interpreters of winds. They are mighty waving goldenrods, ever in tune, singing and writing wind-music all their long century lives.

The Mountains of California

[F]ew indeed, strong and free with eyes undimmed with care, have gone far enough and lived long enough with the trees to gain anything like a loving conception of their grandeur and significance as manifested in the harmonies of their distribution and varying aspects throughout the seasons, as they stand arrayed in their winter garb rejoicing in storms, putting forth their fresh leaves in the spring while steaming with resiny fragrance, receiving the thundershowers of summer, or reposing heavy-laden with ripe cones in the rich sun-gold of autumn. For knowledge of this kind one must dwell with the trees and grow with them, without any reference to time in the almanac sense.

The Mountains of California

Any fool can destroy trees. They cannot run away; and if they could, they would still be destroyed — chased and hunted down as long as fun or a dollar could be got out of their bark hides, branching horns, or magnificent bole backbones. Few that fell trees plant them; nor would planting avail much towards getting back anything like the noble primeval forests. During a man's life only saplings can be grown, in the place of the old trees — tens of centuries old — that have been destroyed. It took more than three thousand years to make some of the trees in these Western woods — trees that are still standing in perfect strength and beauty, waving and singing in the mighty forests of the Sierra. Through all the wonderful, eventful centuries since Christ's time — and long before that — God has cared for these trees, saved them from drought, disease, avalanches, and a thousand straining, leveling tempests and floods; but he cannot save them from fools — only Uncle Sam can do that.

Our National Parks

Left and opposite:
Towering trees in Yosemite Valley, California.

To learn how trees live in pure wilderness, to see
their varying aspects — for this you must love them . . .

The forests of America, however slighted by man, must have been a great delight to God; for they were the best he ever planted.

Our National Parks

[T]o learn how they [trees] live and behave in pure wildness, to see them in their varying aspects through the seasons and weather, rejoicing in the great storms, in the spiritual mountain light, putting forth their new leaves and flowers when all the streams are in flood and the birds are singing, and sending away their seeds in the thoughtful Indian summer when all the landscape is glowing in deep calm enthusiasm — for this you must love them and live with them, as free from schemes and cares and time as the trees themselves.

Our National Parks

As twilight began to fall, I sat down on the mossy instep of a spruce. Not a bush or tree was moving; every leaf seemed hushed in brooding repose. One bird, a thrush, embroidered the silence with cheery notes, making the solitude familiar and sweet, while the solemn monotone of the stream sifting through the woods seemed like the very voice of God, humanized, terrestrialized, and entering one's heart as to a home prepared for it. Go where we will, all the world over, we seem to have been there before.

Travels in Alaska

On the mossy trunk of an old prostrate spruce about a hundred feet in length thousands of seedlings were growing. I counted seven hundred on a length of eight feet, so favorable is this climate for the development of tree seeds and so fully do these trees obey the command to multiply and replenish the earth.

Travels in Alaska

Walk in the sequoia woods at any time of the year and you will say they are the most beautiful and majestic on earth.

The Mountains of California

Opposite: Redwood tree, California.
Below: A painting of John Muir.

[I]t is not easy to account for the colossal size of the sequoias. The largest are about three hundred feet high, and thirty feet in diameter. Who of all the dwellers of the plains and prairies and fertile home forests of roundheaded oak and maple, hickory and elm, ever dreamed that earth could bear such growths? — trees that the familiar pines and firs seem to know nothing about, lonely, silent, serene, with a physiognomy almost godlike, and so old, thousands of them still living had already counted their years by tens of centuries when Columbus set sail from Spain, and were in the vigor of youth or middle age when the star led the Chaldean sages to the infant Savior's cradle. As far as man is concerned, they are the same yesterday, today, and forever, emblems of permanence.

No description can give any adequate idea of their singular majesty, much less of their beauty.... Only in youth does it show, like other conifers, a heavenward yearning, keenly aspiring with a long quick-growing top. Indeed the whole tree, for the first century or two, or until a hundred to a hundred and fifty feet high, is arrowhead in form, and, compared with the solemn rigidity of age, is as sensitive to the wind as a squirrel's tail. The lower branches are gradually dropped as it grows older, and the upper ones thinned out, until comparatively few are left. These, however, are developed to a great size, divide again and again, and terminate in bossy rounded masses of leafy branchlets, while the head is dome-shaped. Then poised in fullness of strength and beauty, stern and solemn in mien, it glows with eager, enthusiastic life, quivering to the tip of every leaf and branch and far-reaching root, calm as a granite dome — the first to feel the touch of the rosy beams of the morning, the last to bid the sun good night.

...It is a curious fact that all the very old sequoias have lost their head by lightning. "All things come to him who waits;" but of all living things Sequoia is perhaps the only one able to wait long enough to make sure of being struck by lightning. Thousands of years it stands ready and waiting, offering its head to every passing cloud as if inviting its fate, praying for heaven's fire as a blessing; and when at last the old head is off, another of the same shape immediately begins to grow on. Every bud and branch seems exciting, like bees that have lost their queen, and tries hard to repair the damage. Branches that for many centuries have been growing out horizontally at once turn upward, and all their branchlets arrange themselves with reference to a new top of the same peculiar curve as the old one. Even the small subordinate branches halfway down the trunk do their best to push up to the top and help in this curious head-making.

"Hunting Big Redwoods," *The Atlantic Monthly*
September 1901

The entrance to Yosemite Valley, with El Capitan
at left and Bridalveil Fall at right.

Ed Cooper

[A]bout two hours after beginning the descent, we found ourselves among the sugar pine groves at the lower end of the valley, through which we rode in perfect ecstasy, for never did pines seem so noble and religious in all their gestures and tones. The sun pouring down mellow gold, seemed to be shining only for them, and the wind gave them voice, but the gestures of their outstretched arms appeared wholly independent of the winds, and impressed one with a solemn awe that overbore all our knowledge of causes and brought us into the condition of beings new-arrived from some other far-off world. The ground was smoothly strewn with dead, clean leaves and burs, making a fine brown surface for shadows, many a wide even bar, from tapering trunk columns, and rich mosaic from living leaf and branch. There amid the groves we came to small openings without a tree or shadow, wholly filled with the sun like poles of glowing light. . . .

Our ride up the valley was perfectly enchanting, every bend of the river presenting reaches of surpassing loveliness, sunbeams streaming thorugh its border groves, or falling in broad masses upon the white rapids or calm, deep pools. Here and there a dead pine that had been swept down in flood time reached out over the current, its green mosses and lichens contrasting with the crystal sheen of the water, and its gnarled roots forming shadowy caves for speckled trout where the current eddies slowly, and protecting sedges and willows dip their leaves. Among these varied and ever-changing river reaches the appreciative artist may find studies for a lifetime.

San Francisco Daily Evening Bulletin
August 13, 1875

No lover of trees will ever forget his first meeting with the sugar pine, nor will he afterward need a poet to call him to "listen what the pine tree saith." In most pine trees there is a sameness of expression, which, to most people, is apt to become monotonous; for the typical spiry form, however beautiful, affords but little scope for appreciably individual character. The sugar pine is as free from conventionalities of form and motion as any oak. No two are alike, even to the most inattentive observer; and, notwithstanding they are ever tossing out their immense arms in what might seem most extravagant gestures, there is a majesty and repose about them that precludes all possibility of the grotesque, or even picturesque, in their general expression. They are the priests of pines, and seem ever to be addressing the surrounding forest. . . .

No other pine seems to me so unfamiliar and self-contained. In approaching it, we feel as if in the presence of a superior being, and begin to walk with a light step, holding our breath. Then, perchance, while we gaze awe-stricken, along comes a merry squirrel, chattering and laughing, to break the spell, running up the trunk with no ceremony, and gnawing off the cones as if they were made

Ed Cooper

Cascading stream, Sierra Nevada.

only for him; while the carpenter woodpecker hammers away at the bark, drilling holes in which to store his winter supply of acorns.

Although so wild and unconventional when full-grown, the sugar pine is a remarkably proper tree in youth. The old is the most original and independent in appearance of all the Sierra evergreens; the young is the most regular — a strict follower of coniferous fashions — slim, erect, with leafy, supple branches kept exactly in place, each tapering in outline and terminating in a spiry point. The successive transitional forms presented between the cautious neatness of youth and bold freedom of maturity offer a delightful study. At the age of fifty or sixty years, the shy, fashionable form begins to be broken up. Specialized branches push out in the most unthought-of places, and bend with the great cones, at once marking individual character, and this being constantly augmented from year to year by the varying action of the sunlight, winds, snow-storms, etc., the individuality of the tree is never again lost in the general forest.

The Mountains of California

31

I will climb every mountain . . .

A Steller's jay in the Sierras, California.

Nearly all my mountaineering has been done on foot, carrying as little as possible, depending on camp-fires for warmth, that so I might be light and free to go wherever my studies might lead.

Our National Parks

I saw no mountains in all this grand region that appeared at all inaccessible to a mountaineer. Give me a summer and a bunch of matches and a sack of meal and I will climb every mountain in the region.

Letter to Mrs. Ezra S. Carr
October 17, 1873

Falling rocks, single or in avalanches, form the greatest of all the perils that beset the mountaineer among the summit peaks.

San Francisco Daily Evening Bulletin
August 24, 1875

Ed Cooper

A wind-shaped Jeffrey pine overlooks
Half Dome and Yosemite Valley, Sierras.

...Then the rain began to abate and I sauntered down through the dripping bushes reveling in the universal vigor and freshness that inspired all the life about me. How clean and unworn and immortal the woods seemed to be! — the lofty cedars in full bloom laden with golden pollen and their washed plumes shining; the pines rocking gently and settling back into rest, and the evening sunbeams spangling on the broad leaves of the madroños, their tracery of yellow boughs relieved against dusky thickets of chestnut oak; liverworts, lycopodiums, ferns were exulting in glorious revival, and every moss that had ever lived seemed to be coming crowding back from the dead to clothe each trunk and stone in living green. The steaming ground seemed fairly to throb and tingle with life; smilax, fritillaria, saxifrage, and young violets were pushing up as if already conscious of the summer glory, and innumerable green and yellow buds were peeping and smiling everywhere.

The Mountains of California

33

Snowfall along the Merced River, Sierra Nevada.

Ed Cooper

The noble trees stand hushed . . .

...The rain brought out the colors of the woods with delightful freshness, the rich brown of the bark of the trees and the fallen burs and leaves and dead ferns; the grays of rocks and lichens; the light purple of swelling buds, and the warm yellow greens of the libocedrus and mosses. The air was steaming with delightful fragrance, not rising and wafting past in separate masses, but diffused through all the atmosphere. Pine woods are always fragrant, but most so in spring when the young tassels are opening and in warm weather when the various gums and balsams are softened by the sun. The wind was now chafing their innumerable needles and the warm rain was steeping them. Monardella grows here in large beds in the openings, and there is plenty of laurel in dells and manzanita on the hillsides, and the rosy, fragrant chamoebatia carpets the ground almost everywhere. These, with the gums and balsams of the woods, form the main local fragrance-fountains of the storm.

The Mountains of California

The greatest [snow] storms, however, are usually followed by a deep, peculiar silence, especially profound and solemn in the forests; and the noble trees stand hushed and motionless, as if under a spell, until the morning sunbeams begin to sift through their laden spires.

Our National Parks

The mountain winds, like the dew and rain, sunshine and snow, are measured and bestowed with love on the forests to develop their strength and beauty. However restricted the scope of other forest influences, that of the winds is universal. The snow bends and trims the upper forests every winter, the lightning strikes a single tree here and there, while avalanches mow down thousands at a swoop as a gardner trims out a bed of flowers. But the winds go to every tree, fingering every leaf and branch and furrowed bole; not one is forgotten; the mountain pine towering with outstretched arms on the rugged buttresses of the icy peaks; the lowliest and most retiring tenant of the dells; they seek and find them all, caressing them tenderly, bending them in lusty exercise, stimulating their growth, plucking off a leaf or limb as required, or removing an entire tree or grove, now whispering and cooing through the branches like a sleepy child, now roaring like the ocean; the winds blessing the forests, the forests the winds, with ineffable beauty and harmony as a sure result.

The Mountains of California

Ice decorates Upper Yosemite Falls, Sierras.

35

The winds finger the mountain pines towering with outstretched arms on the buttresses of icy peaks. . .

In Yosemite Valley, one morning about two o'clock, I was aroused by an earthquake; and though I had never before enjoyed a storm of this sort, the strange, wild thrilling motion and rumbling could not be mistaken, and I ran out of my cabin, near the Sentinel Rock, both glad and frightened, shouting, "A noble earthquake!" feeling sure I was going to learn something. The shocks were so violent and varied, and succeeded one another so closely, one had to balance in walking as if on the deck of a ship among the waves, and it seemed impossible the high cliffs should escape being shattered. In particular, I feared that the sheer-fronted Sentinel Rock, which rises to a height of three thousand feet, would be shaken down, and I took shelter back of a big pine, hoping I might be protected from outbounding boulders, should any come so far. I was now convinced that an earthquake had been the maker of the taluses, and positive proof soon came. It was a calm moonlight night, and no sound was heard for the first minute or two save a low muffled underground rumbling and a slight rustling of the agitated trees, as if, in wrestling with the mountains, Nature were holding her breath. Then, suddenly, out of the strange silence and strange motion, there came a tremendous roar. The Eagle Rock, a short distance up the valley, had given way, and I saw it falling in thousands of the great boulders I had been studying so long, pouring to the valley floor in a free curve luminous from friction, making a terribly sublime and beautiful spectacle — an arc of fire fifteen hundred feet span, as true in form and as steady as a rainbow, in the midst of the stupendous roaring rock storm. The sound was inconceivably deep and broad and earnest, as if the whole earth, like a living creature, had at last found a voice and were calling to her sister planets. It seemed to me that if all the thunder I ever heard were condensed into one roar it would not equal this rock roar at the birth of a mountain talus.

Our National Parks

Ancient bristlecone pine in the White Mountains, California.

Shadows crept out across the snow . . .

In the morning everything is joyous and bright, the delicious purple of the dawn changes softly to daffodil yellow and white; while the sunbeams pouring the passes between the peaks give a margin of gold to each of them. Then the spires of the firs in the hollows of the middle region catch the glow, and your camp grove is filled with light. The birds begin the stir, seeking sunny branches on the edge of the meadow for sun-baths after the cold night, and looking for their breakfasts, every one of them as fresh as a lily and as charmingly arrayed.

The Mountains of California

The sunbeams streaming through their [trees'] feather arches brighten the ground, and you walk beneath the radiant ceiling in devout subdued mood, as if you were in a grand cathedral with mellow light sifting through colored windows, while the flowery pillared aisles open enchanting vistas in every direction.

Our National Parks

The nearer peaks are perchance clad in sapphire blue, others far off in creamy white. In the broad glare of noon they seem to shrink and crouch to less than half their real stature, and grow dull and uncommunicative — mere dead, draggled heaps of waste ashes and stone, giving no hint of the multitude of animals enjoying life in their fastnesses, or of the bright bloom-bordered streams and lakes. But when storms blow they awake and arise, wearing robes of cloud and mist in majestic speaking attitudes like gods. In the color glory of morning and evening they become still more imperssive; steeped in the divine light of the alpenglow their earthiness disappears, and, blending with the heavens, they seem neither high nor low.

Our National Parks

Now came the solemn, silent evening. Long, blue, spiky shadows crept out across the snow-fields, while a rosy glow, at first scarce discernible, gradually deepened and suffused every mountain-top, flushing the glaciers and the harsh crags above them. This was the alpenglow, to me one of the most impressive of all the terrestrial manifestations of God. At the touch of this divine light, the mountains seemed to kindle to a rapt, religious consciousness, and stood hushed and waiting like devout worshipers.

The Mountains of California

Ed Cooper

Mounts Winchell and Agassiz in the Sierras.

[A]s I gazed every color seemed to deepen and glow as if the progress of the fresh sun-work were visible from hour to hour, while every tree seemed religious and conscious of the presence of God.

Our National Parks

The evening flames with purple and gold. The breeze that has been blowing from the lowlands dies away, and far and near the mighty host of trees baptizes in the purple flood stand hushed and thoughtful, awaiting the sun's blessing and farewell — as impressive a ceremony as if it were never to rise again.

Our National Parks

Ted Czolowski from Quest Travelbooks Ltd.

40

Glaciers flowing into Glacier Bay along Alaska's southeastern coast.

I caught the big bright eyes of a deer gazing at me...

Beneath the frost shadows of the fiord we stood hushed and awe stricken, gazing at the holy vision; and had we seen the heavens opened and God made manifest, our attention could not have been more tremendously strained.... Peak after peak ... caught the heavenly glow, until all the mighty host stood transfigured, hushed and thoughtful, as if awaiting the coming of the Lord. The white, rayless light of morning, seen when I was alone amid the peaks of the California Sierra, had always seemed to me the most telling of all the terrestrial manifestations of God. But here the mountains themselves were made divine, and declared His glory in terms still more impressive.... We turned and sailed away, joining the outgoing bergs, while "Gloria in excelsis" still seemed to be sounding over all the white landscape, and our burning hearts were ready for any fate, feeling that, whatever the future might have in store, the treasures we had gained this glorious morning would enrich our lives forever.

Travels in Alaska

[S]unshine streamed through the luminous fringes of the clouds and fell on the green waters of the fiord, the glittering bergs, and the crystal bluffs of the vast glacier, the intensely white, far-spreading fields of ice, and the ineffably chaste and spiritual heights of the Fairweather Range, which were now hidden, now partly revealed, the whole making a picture of icy wilderness unspeakably pure and sublime.

Travels in Alaska

... [S]hortly after sunrise, just as the light was beginning to come streaming through the trees, while I lay leaning on my elbow taking my bread and tea, and looking down across the cañon, tracing the hip of the granite headlands, and trying to plan a way to the river at a point likely to be fordable, suddenly I caught the big bright eyes of a deer gazing at me through the garden hedge. The expressive eyes, the slim black-tipped muzzle, and the large ears were as perfectly visible as if placed there at just the right distance to be seen, like a picture on the wall. She continued to gaze, while I gazed back with equal steadiness, motionless as a rock. In a few minutes she ventured forward a step, exposing her fine arching neck and forelegs, then snorted and withdrew.

This alone was a fine picture — the beautiful eyes framed in colored cherry leaves, the topmost sprays lightly atremble, and just glanced by the level sunrays, all the rest in shadow.

"The New Sequoia Forests of California,"
Harper's Monthly, November 1878

National Park Service, Keller

Above: Mule deer in Dinosaur National Monument, Colorado-Utah.
Below: A female sage grouse blends well into the environment.

National Park Service, Keller

Alpine lake, Sierra Nevada.

Deer are capital mountaineers, making their way into the heart of the roughest mountains; seeking not only pasturage, but a cool climate, and safe hidden places in which to bring forth their young.

Our National Parks

The Douglas squirrel is by far the most interesting and influential of the California sciuridae, surpassing every other species in force of character, numbers, and extent of range, and in the amount of influence he brings to bear upon the health and distribution of the vast forests he inhabits. . . .

I cannot begin to tell here how much he has cheered my lonely wanderings during all the years I have been pursuing my studies in these glorious wilds; or how much unmistakable humanity I have found in him.

The Mountains of California

The tendency nowadays to wander in wildernesses is delightful to see. Thousands of tired, nerve-shaken, over-civilized people are beginning to find out that going to the mountains is going home; that wildness is a necessity; and that mountain parks and reservations are useful not only as fountains of timber and irrigating rivers, but as fountains of life. Awakening from the stupefying effects of the vice of over-industry and the deadly apathy of luxury, they are trying as best they can to mix and enrich their own little ongoings with those of Nature, and to get rid of rust and disease. Briskly venturing and roaming, some are washing off sins and cobweb cares of the devil's spinning in all-day storms on mountains; sauntering in resiny pinewoods or in gentian meadow, brushing through chaparral, bending down and parting sweet, flowery sprays; tracing rivers to their sources, getting in touch with the nerves of Mother Earth; jumping from rock to rock, feeling the life of them, learning the songs of them, panting in whole-souled exercise, and rejoicing in deep, long-drawn breaths of pure wildness. This is fine and natural and full of promise.

Our National Parks

As age comes on, one source of enjoyment after another is closed, but Nature's sources never fail. Like a generous host, she offers her brimming cups in endless variety, served in a grand hall, the sky its ceiling, the mountains its walls, decorated with bands of music ever playing. The petty discomforts that beset the awkward guest, the unskilled camper, are quickly forgotten, while all that is precious remains. Fears vanish as soon as one is fairly free in the wilderness.

Our National Parks

Deception Creek in the Cascade Mountains, Washington.

Ed Cooper

45

The Colorado River courses through its sculpted
masterpiece, the Grand Canyon, Arizona.

The Grand Cañon is incomparably lovely, supreme above all cañons . . .

No matter how far you have wandered hitherto, or how many famous gorges and valleys you have seen, this one, the Grand Cañon of the Colorado, will seem as novel to you, as unearthly in the color and grandeur and quantity of its architecture, as if you had found it after death, on some other star; so incomparably lovely and grand and supreme is it above all the other cañons in our fire-moulded, earthquake-shaken, rain-washed, wave-washed, river and glacier sculptured world. It is about six thousand feet deep where you first see it, and from rim to rim ten to fifteen miles wide. Instead of being dependent for interest upon waterfalls, depth, wall sculpture, and beauty of parklike floor, like most other great canons, it has no waterfalls in sight, and no appreciable floor spaces. The big river has just room enough to flow and roar obscurely, here and there groping its way as best it can, like a weary, murmuring, overladen traveler trying to escape from the tremendous, bewildering labyrinthic abyss, while its roar serves only to deepen the silence.

Our National Parks

None of Nature's landscapes are ugly so long as they are wild; and much, we can say comfortingly, must always be in the great part wild, particularly the sea and the sky, the floods of light from the stars, and the warm, un-spoilable heart of the earth, infinitely beautiful, though only dimly visible to the eye of imagination. The geysers, too, spouting from the hot underworld; the steady, long-lasting glaciers on the mountains, obedient only to the sun; Yosemite domes and the tremendous grandeur of rocky cañons and mountains in general — these must always be wild, for man can change them and mar them hardly more than can the butterflies that hover above them. But the continent's outer beauty is fast passing away, especially the plant part of it, the most destructible and the most univer-sally charming of all.

Our National Parks

Overleaf: Tall pines form a canopy, Sierras, California.

JOHN BURROUGHS

III Wilds Along the Hudson

When I want the wild of a little different flavor and quality from that immediately about my cabin, I go a mile through the woods to Black Creek, here called the Shattega, and put my canoe into a long, smooth, silent stretch of water that winds through a heavily timbered marsh till it leads into Black Pond, an oval sheet of water half a mile or more across. Here I get the moist, spongy, tranquil, luxurious side of Nature. Here she stands or sits knee-deep in water, and wreathes herself with pond lilies in summer, and bedecks herself with scarlet maples in autumn. She is an Indian maiden, dark, subtle, dreaming, with glances now and then that thrill the wild blood in one's veins. The Shattega here is a stream without banks and with a just perceptible current. It is a waterway through a timbered marsh. The level floor of the woods ends in an irregular line where the level surface of the water begins. As one glides along in his boat, he sees various rank aquatic growths slowly waving in the shadowy depths beneath him. The larger trees on each side unite their branches above his head, so that at times he seems to be entering an arboreal cave out of which glides the stream. In the more open places the woods mirror themselves in the glassy surface till one seems floating between two worlds, clouds and sky and trees below him matching those around and above him. A bird flits from shore to shore, and one sees it duplicated against the sky in the under-world. What vistas open! What banks of drooping foliage, what grain and arch of gnarled branches, lure the eye as one drifts or silently paddles along!

Far and Near

Opposite: Autumn colors at a New England lake. Burroughs was content to view the passing of the seasons in the Catskill Mountains.
Right: Burroughs at his summer home near Roxbury, central New York State.

American Museum of Natural History

51

I built me a rustic house
which I call "Slabsides"...

Friends have often asked me why I turned my back upon the Hudson and retreated into the wilderness. Well, I do not call it a retreat; I call it a withdrawal, a retirement, the taking up of a new position to renew the attack, it may be, more vigorously than ever. It is not always easy to give reasons, and often no reasons at all that we are aware of.

To a countryman like myself, not born to a great river or an extensive water view, these things, I think, grow wearisome after a time. He becomes surfeited with a beauty that is alien to him. He longs for something more homely, private, and secluded. Scenery may be too fine or too grand and imposing for one's daily and hourly view. It tires after a while. It demands a mood that comes to you only at intervals. Hence it is never wise to build your house on the most ambitious spot in the landscape. Rather seek out a more humble and secluded nook or corner, which you can fill and warm with your domestic and home instincts and affections. In some things the half is often more satisfying than the whole. A glimpse of the Hudson River between hills or through openings in the trees wears better with me than a long expanse of it constantly spread out before me. One day I had an errand to a farmhouse nestled in a little valley or basin at the foot of a mountain. The earth put out protecting arms all about it—a low hill with an orchard on one side, a sloping pasture on another, and the mountain, with the skirts of its mantling forests, close at hand in the rear. How my heart warmed toward it! I had been so long perched high upon the banks of a great river, in sight of all the world, exposed to every wind that blows, with a horizon line that sweeps over half a county, that, quite unconsciously to myself, I was pining for a nook to sit down in. I was hungry for the private and the circumscribed; I knew it when I saw this sheltered farmstead. I had long been restless and dissatisfied—a vague kind of homesickness; now I knew the remedy. Hence when, not long afterward, I was offered a tract of wild land, barely a mile from home, that contained a secluded nook and a few acres of level, fertile land shut off from the vain and noisy world of railroads, steamboats, and yachts by a wooded, precipitous mountain, I quickly closed the bargain, and built me a rustic house there, which I call "Slabsides" because its outer walls are covered with slabs. I might have given it a prettier name, but not one more fit, or more in keeping with the mood that brought me thither.

Far and Near

Velvet-soft cattail, New England.

Burroughs's retreat, Slabsides, along
the Hudson River in the Catskills.

The power to see straight is the rarest of gifts; to see
no more and no less than is actually before you; to be able to
detach yourself and see the thing as it actually is, uncolored
or unmodified by your own sentiments or prepossessions.
In short, to see with your reason as well as with your
perceptions, that is to be an observer and to read the book
of nature aright.

Ways of Nature

What appears more real than the sky? We think of it
and speak of it as if it was as positive and tangible a fact as
the earth. See how it is painted by the sunset or by the
sunrise. How blue it is by day, how gemmed by stars at
night. At one time tender and wooing, at another hard and
distant. Yet what an illusion! There is no sky; it is only
vacancy, only empty space. It is a glimpse of the infinite.

The Light of Day

53

Pattern of pine needles, northern Michigan.

The friendly and cheering fire, what acquaintance we make with it! . . .

Not the least of the charm of camping out is your campfire at night. What an artist! What pictures are boldly thrown or faintly outlined upon the canvas of the night! Every object, every attitude of your companion, is striking and memorable. You see effects and groups every moment that you would give money to be able to carry away with you in enduring form. How the shadows leap, and skulk, and hover about! Light and darkness are in perpetual tilt and warfare, with first the one unhorsed, then the other. The friendly and cheering fire, what acquaintance we make with it! We had almost forgotten there was such an element, we had so long known only its dark offspring, heat. Now we see the wild beauty uncaged and note its manner and temper. How surely it creates its own draft and sets the currents going, as force and enthusiasm always will! It carves itself a chimney out of the fluid and houseless air. A friend, a ministering angel, in subjection; a fiend, a fury, a monster, ready to devour the world, if ungoverned. By day it burrows in the ashes and sleeps; at night it comes forth and sits upon its throne of rude logs, and rules the camp, a sovereign queen. . .

What does the camper think about when lounging around the fire at night? Not much—of the sport of the day, of the big fish he lost and might have saved, of the distant settlement, of tomorrow's plans. An owl hoots off in the mountain and he thinks of him; if a wolf were to howl or a panther to scream, he would think of him the rest of the night. As it is, things flicker and hover through his mind, and he hardly knows whether it is the past or the present that possesses him. Certain it is, he feels the hush and solitude of the great forest, and, whether he will or not, all his musings are in some way cast upon that huge background of the night.

Locusts and Wild Honey

When one breaks camp in the morning, he turns back again and again to see what he has left. Surely, he feels, he has forgotten something; what is it? But it is only his own sad thoughts and musings he has left, the fragment of his life he has lived there. Where he hung his coat on the tree, where he slept on the boughs, where he made his coffee or broiled his trout over the coals, where he drank again and again at the little brown pool in the spring run, where he looked long and long up into the whispering branches overhead, he has left what he cannot bring away with him—the flame and the ashes of himself.

Pepacton

A campfire throws its light into the
dark woods and offers companionship.

At twilight there was an ominous rumble behind the
mountains. I was on the lake, and could see what was brew-
ing there in the west.

As darkness came on, the rumbling increased, and the
mountains and the woods and the still air were such good
conductors of sound that the ear was vividly impressed.
One seemed to feel the enormous convolutions of the
clouds in the deep and jarring tones of the thunder. The
coming of night in the woods is alone peculiarly impressive,
and it is doubly so when out of the darkness comes such a
voice as this. But we fed the fire the more industriously,
and piled the logs high, and kept the gathering gloom at bay
by as large a circle of light as we could command. The lake
was a pool of ink and as still as if congealed; not a movement or a sound, save now and then a terrific volley from
the cloud batteries now fast approaching. By nine o'clock
little puffs of wind began to steal through the woods and
tease and toy with our fire. Shortly after, an enormous
electric bombshell exploded in the treetops over our heads,

Lightning illuminates the sky in southern Arizona.

Gary Ladd

It was a meteorological carnival and the revelers were drunk with the wild sport . . .

and the ball was fairly opened. Then followed three hours, with only two brief intermissions, of as lively elemental music and as copious an outpouring of rain as it was ever my lot to witness. It was a regular meteorological carnival, and the revelers were drunk with the wild sport. The apparent nearness of the clouds and the electric explosion was something remarkable. Every discharge seemed to be in the branches immediately overhead and made us involuntarily cower, as if the next moment the great limbs of the trees, or the trees themselves, would come crashing down. The mountain upon which we were encamped appeared to be the focus of three distinct but converging storms. The last two seemed to come into collision immediately over our campfire, and to contend for the right of way, until the heavens were ready to fall and both antagonists were literally spent. We stood in groups about the struggling fire, and when the cannonade became too terrible would withdraw into the cover of the darkness, as if to be a less conspicuous mark for the bolts; or did we fear the fire, with its currents, might attract the lightning? At any rate, some other spot than the one where we happened to be standing seemed desirable when those onsets of the contending elements were the most furious. . . .The air was filled with falling water. The sound upon the myriad leaves and branches was like the roar of a cataract. We put our backs up against the great trees, only to catch a brook on our shoulders or in the backs of our necks. Still the storm waxed. The fire was beaten down lower and lower. It surrendered one post after another, like a besieged city, and finally made only a feeble resistance from beneath a pile of charred logs and branches in the center. . . .About midnight the rain slackened, and by one o'clock ceased entirely. How the rest of the night was passed beneath the dripping trees and upon the saturated ground, I have only the dimmest remembrance.

Locusts and Wild Honey

The great bugaboo of the birds is the owl . . .

A robin in early spring, Texas.

John Tveten

It is this period [spring] that marks the return of the birds—one or two of the more hardy or half-domesticated species, like the song sparrow and the bluebird, usually arriving in March, while the rarer and more brilliant wood birds bring up the procession in June. But each stage of the advancing season gives prominence to certain species, as to certain flowers. The dandelion tells me when to look for the swallow, the dogtooth violet when to expect the wood-thrush, and when I have found the wake-robin [trillium] in bloom I know the season is fairly inaugurated. With me this flower is associated, not merely with the awakening of Robin, for he has been awake some weeks, but with the universal awakening and rehabilitation of nature.

Yet the coming and going of the birds is more or less a mystery and a surprise. We go out in the morning, and no thrush or vireo is to be heard; we go out again, and every tree and grove is musical; yet again, and all is silent. Who saw them come? Who saw them depart?

This pert little winter wren, for instance, darting in and out the fence, diving under the rubbish here and coming up yards away—how does he manage with those little circular wings to compass degrees and zones, and arrive always in the nick of time? . . .

And yonder bluebird with the earth tinge on his breast and the sky tinge on his back—did he come down out of heaven on that bright March morning when he told us so softly and plaintively that, if we pleased, spring had come? . . . The bird at first seems a mere wandering voice in the air; one hears its call or carol on some bright March morning, but is uncertain of its source or direction; it falls like a drop of rain when no cloud is visible; one looks and listens, but to no purpose. The weather changes, perhaps a cold snap with snow comes on, and it may be a week before I hear the note again, and this time or the next perchance I see the bird sitting on a stake in the fence lifting his wing as he calls cheerily to his mate. Its notes now become daily more frequent; the birds multiply, and, flitting from point to point, call and warble more confidently and gleefully. . . .

Not long after the bluebird comes the robin, sometimes in March, but in most of the Northern states April is the month of the robin. In large numbers they scour the fields and groves. You hear their piping in the meadow, in the pasture, on the hillside. Walk in the woods, and the dry leaves rustle with the whir of their wings, the air is vocal with their cheery call. In excess of joy and vivacity, they run, leap, scream, chase each other through the air, diving and sweeping among the trees with perilous rapidity.

Wake-Robin

An owl spreads his wings, Wisconsin.

I find I see, almost without effort, nearly every bird within sight in the field or wood I pass through (a flit of the wing, a flirt of the tail are enough, though the flickering leaves do all conspire to hide them), and that with like ease the birds see me, though, unquestionably, the chances are immensely in their favor. The eye sees what it has the means of seeing, truly. You must have the bird in your heart before you find it in the bush.

Locusts and Wild Honey

The great bugaboo of the birds is the owl. The owl snatches them from off their roosts at night, and gobbles up their eggs and young in their nests. He is a veritable ogre to them, and his presence fills them with consternation and alarm.

Signs and Seasons

59

Reflecting colors in Cascade Pond,
Adirondacks, upstate New York.

Spring is the inspiration, fall the expiration. Both seasons have their equinoxes, both their filmy, hazy air, their ruddy forest tints, their cold rains, their drenching fogs, their mystic moons; both have the same solar light and warmth, the same rays of the sun; yet, after all, how different the feelings which they inspire! One is the morning, the other the evening; one is youth, the other is age. . . .

It is rarely that an artist succeeds in painting unmistakably the difference between sunrise and sunset; and it is equally a trial of his skill to put upon canvas the difference between early spring and late fall, say between April and November. It was long ago observed that the shadows are more opaque in the morning than in the evening; the struggle between the light and the darkness more marked, the gloom more solid, the contrasts more sharp, etc. The rays of the morning sun chisel out and cut down the shadows in a way those of the setting sun do not. Then the sunlight is whiter and newer in the morning—not so yellow and diffused. A difference akin to this is true of the two seasons I am speaking of. The spring is the morning sunlight, clear and determined; the autumn, the afternoon rays, pensive, lessening, golden.

Winter Sunshine

60

The fall of '74 was the most remarkable . . . I remember ever to have seen. The equilibrium of the season lasted from the middle of October till near December, with scarcely a break. There were six weeks of Indian summer, all gold by day, and, when the moon came, all silver by night. The river was so smooth at times as to be almost invisible, and in its place was the indefinite continuation of the opposite shore down toward the nether world. One seemed to be in an enchanted land, and to breathe all day the atmosphere of fable and romance. Not a smoke, but a kind of shining nimbus filled all the spaces. The vessels would drift by as if in mid-air with all their sails set. The gypsy blood in one, as Lowell calls it, could hardly stay between four walls and see such days go by. Living in tents, in groves and on the hills, seemed the only natural life.

Winter Sunshine

Both the pine and the hemlock make friends with the birch, the maple, and the oak, and one of the most pleasing and striking features of our autumnal scenery is a mountainside sown broadcast with these intermingled trees, forming a combination of colors like the richest tapestry, the dark green giving body and permanence, the orange and yellow giving light and brilliancy.

Signs and Seasons

The country is more of a wilderness, more of a wild solitude, in the winter than in the summer. The wild comes out. The urban, the cultivated, is hidden or negatived. You shall hardly know a good field from a poor, a meadow from a pasture, a park from a forest. Lines and boundaries are disregarded; gates and barways are unclosed; man lets go his hold upon the earth; title deeds are deep buried beneath the snow; the best-kept grounds relapse to a state of nature; under the pressure of the cold all the wild creatures become outlaws, and roam abroad beyond their usual haunts. The partridge comes to the orchard for buds; the rabbit comes to the garden and lawn; the crows and jays come to the ash heap and corncrib, the snow buntings to the stack and to the barnyard; the sparrows pilfer from the domestic fowls; the pine grosbeak comes down from the north and shears your maples of their buds; the fox prowls about your premises at night, and the red squirrels find your grain in the barn or steal the butternuts from your attic. In fact, winter, like some great calamity, changes the status of most creatures and sets them adrift. Winter, like poverty, makes us acquainted with strange bedfollows.

Signs and Seasons

Leaf on a bed of moss, northern Michigan.

Robert Carr

61

*A fall of snow, and this
icy uproar is instantly hushed,
the river sleeps in peace . . .*

All sounds are sharper in winter; the air transmits better. At night I hear more distinctly the steady roar of the North Mountain. In summer it is a sort of complacent purr, as the breezes stroke down its sides; but in winter always the same low, sullen growl.

A severe artist! No longer the canvas and the pigments, but the marble and the chisel. When the nights are calm and the moon full, I go out to gaze upon the wonderful purity of the moonlight and the snow. The air is full of latent fire, and the cold warms me—after a different fashion from that of the kitchen stove. The world lies about me in a "trance of snow." The clouds are pearly and iridescent, and seem the farthest possible remove from the condition of a storm—the ghosts of clouds, the indwelling beauty freed from all dross. I see the hills, bulging with great drifts, lift themselves up cold and white against the sky, the black lines of fences here and there obliterated by the depth of the snow. Presently a fox barks away up next the mountain, and I imagine I can almost see him sitting there, in his furs, upon the illuminated surface, and looking down in my direction. As I listen, one answers him from behind the woods in the valley. What a wild winter sound, wild and weird, up among the ghostly hills!

Winter Sunshine

A fall of snow, and this icy uproar [Hudson River] is instantly hushed, the river sleeps in peace. The snow is like a coverlid, which protects the ice from the changes of temperature of the air, and brings repose to its uneasy spirit.

Signs and Seasons

Look up at the miracle of the falling snow—the air a dizzy maze of whirling, eddying flakes, noiselessly transforming the world, the exquisite crystals dropping in ditch and gutter, and disguising in the same suit of spotless livery all objects upon which they fall.

Winter Sunshine

The Hudson River and the Catskills near Burroughs's home, Riverby, West Park, New York.

Gary Randorf

Above: Sentinel Range in the Adirondacks, near Lake Placid, upstate New York.
Opposite: Melting snow provides needed moisture to plants for spring growth.

The snow-walkers are mostly night-walkers also, and the record they leave upon the snow is the main clew one has to their life and doings. . . .

The sharp-rayed track of the partridge adds another figure to this fantastic embroidery upon the winter snow. Her course is a clear, strong line, sometimes quite wayward, but generally very direct, steering for the densest, most impenetrable places — leading you over logs and through brush, alert and expectant, till, suddenly, she bursts up a few yards from you, and goes humming through the trees — the complete triumph of endurance and vigor.

Winter Sunshine

One may walk for hours through the winter woods and not see or hear a bird. Then he may come upon a troop of chickadees, with a nuthatch or two in their wake, and maybe a downy woodpecker. Birds not of a feather flock together at this inclement season. The question of food is always an urgent one. Evidently the nuthatch thinks there must be food where the chickadees flit and call so cheerily, and the woodpecker is probably drawn to the nuthatch for a simliar reason.

Far and Near

65

This lady's slipper is one of the rarest of our wild flowers. . .

All beginnings in nature afford us a peculiar pleasure. The early spring with its hints and dim prophecies, the first earth odors, the first robin or song sparrow, the first furrow, the first tender skies, the first rainbow, the first wild flower, the dropping bud scales, the awakening voices in the marshes — all these things touch and move us in a way that later developments in the season do not.

Literary Values

One sometimes seems to discover a familiar wild flower anew by coming upon it in some peculiar and striking situation. Our columbine is at all times and in all places one of the most exquisitely beautiful of flowers; yet one spring day, when I saw it growing out of a small seam on the face of a great lichen-covered wall of rock, where no soil or mould was visible — a jet of foliage and color shooting out of a black line on the face of a perpendicular mountain wall and rising up like a tiny fountain, its drops turning to flame-colored jewels that hung and danced in the air against the gray rocky surface — its beauty became something magical and audacious.

Riverby

There are many things left for May, but nothing fairer, if as fair, as the first flower, the hepatica. I find I have never admired this little firstling half enough. When at the maturity of its charm, it is certainly the gem of the woods. What an individuality it has ! No two clusters alike; all shades and sizes; some are snow-white, some pale pink, with just a tinge of violet, some deep purple, others the purest blue, others blue touched with lilac. A solitary blue-purple one, fully expanded and rising over the brown leaves or the green moss, its cluster of minute anthers showing like a group of pale stars on its little firmament, is enough to arrest and hold the dullest eye.

Signs and Seasons

This lady's slipper is one of the rarest and choicest of our wild flowers, and its haunts and its beauty are known only to the few. . . .

Report had come to me, through my botanizing neighbor, that in a certain quaking sphagnum bog in the woods the showy lady's slipper could be found. The locality proved to be the marrowy grave of an extinct lake or black tarn. On the borders of it the white azalea was in bloom, fast fading. In the midst of it were spruces and black ash giant ferns, and, low in the spongy, mossy bottom, the pitcher plant. The lady's slipper grew in little groups and companies all about. Never have I beheld a prettier sight — so gay, so festive, so holiday-looking.

Riverby

The sight of a delicate lady's slipper excited Burroughs.

John Tveten

Hepatica blossoms reach for the sunlight, upstate New York.

Our next move was a tramp of about twelve miles through the [Adirondack] wilderness, most of the way in a drenching rain, to a place called the Lower Iron Works, situated on the road leading in to Long Lake . . . .

On the afternoon of our arrival, and also the next morning, the view was completely shut off by the fog. But about the middle of the forenoon the wind changed, the fog lifted and revealed to us the grandest mountain scenery we had beheld on our journey. There they sat about fifteen miles distant, a group of them — Mount Marcy, Mount McIntyre, and Mount Colden, the real Adirondack monarchs. It was an impressive sight, rendered doubly so by the sudden manner in which it was revealed to us by that scene-shifter the Wind.

I saw blackbirds at this place, and sparrows, and the solitary sandpiper, and the Canada woodpecker, and a large number of hummingbirds. Indeed, I saw more of the latter here than I ever before saw in any one locality. Their squeaking and whirring were almost incessant . . . .

About half a mile northeast of the village is Lake Henderson, a very irregular and picturesque sheet of water, surrounded by dark evergreen forests, and abutted by two or three bold promontories with mottled white and gray rocks. Its greatest extent in any one direction is perhaps less than a mile. Its waters are perfectly clear and abound in lake trout. A considerable stream flows into it which comes down from Indian Pass.

A mile south of the village is Lake Sanford. This is a more open and exposed sheet of water and much larger. From some parts of it Mount Marcy and the gorge of the Indian Pass are seen to excellent advantage. The Indian Pass shows as a huge cleft in the mountain, the gray walls rising on one side perpendicularly for many hundred feet.

Wake-Robin

Nature has, for the most part, lost her delicate tints in August. She is tanned, hirsute, freckled, like one long exposed to the sun. Her touch is strong and vivid. The coarser, commoner wayside flowers now appear — vervain, eupatorium, mimulus, the various mints, asters, goldenrod, thistles, fireweed, mulleins, motherwort, catnip, blueweed, turtlehead, sunflowers, clematis, evening primrose, lobelia, gerardia, and, in the marshes of the lower Hudson, marshmallows, and vast masses of the purple loosestrife. Mass and intensity take the place of delicacy and furtiveness. The spirit of Nature has grown bold and aggressive; it is rank and coarse; she flaunts her weeds in our faces. She wears a thistle on her bosom.

Far and Near

G. C. Kelley

Above: A red fox, Alaska, distinguished from the gray fox by its white tail tip. *Opposite:* Bingham Falls at Smugglers Notch, near Stowe, Vermont.

69

Wilford L. Miller

Buffalo along the Little Missouri River, North Dakota's badlands. Roosevelt
liked the frontier life in this region and explored the northern plains at length.
The numbers of buffalo decreased dramatically at the close of the 1800's and Roosevelt
was greatly concerned that this noble animal would disappear altogether.

THEODORE ROOSEVELT

IV The Conservationist President

For a number of years much of my life was spent either in the wilderness or on the borders of the settled country — if, indeed, "settled" is a term that can rightly be applied to the vast, scantily peopled regions where cattle-ranching is the only regular industry. During this time I hunted much, among the mountains and on the plains, both as a pastime and to procure hides, meat, and robes for use on the ranch. . . .

The free, self-reliant, adventurous life, with its rugged and stalwart democracy; the wild surroundings, the grand beauty of the scenery, the chance to study the ways and habits of the woodland creatures — all these unite to give to the career of the wilderness hunter its peculiar charm.

In after years there shall come forever to his mind the memory of endless prairies shimmering in the bright sun; of vast snow-clad wastes lying desolate under gray skies; of the melancholy marshes; of the rush of mighty rivers; of the breath of the evergreen forest in summer; of the crooning of ice-armored pines at the touch of the winds of winter; of cataracts roaring between hoary mountain masses; of all the innumerable sights and sounds of the wilderness; of its immensity and mystery; and of the silences that brood in its still depths.

The Wilderness Hunter

U. S. Department of Agriculture

Roosevelt at Yosemite Valley in 1903, on a visit with John Muir.

71

John Allen, Cyr Agency

A buffalo at the National Bison Range, Montana, established for the preservation of this once nearly extinct species.

Though I had previously made a trip into the then Territory of Dakota, beyond the Red River, it was not until 1883 that I went to the Little Missouri, and there took hold of two cattle-ranches, the Chimney Butte and the Elkhorn.

It was still the Wild West in those days, the far West, the West of Owen Wister's stories and Frederic Remington's drawings, the West of the Indian and the buffalo-hunter, the soldier and the cow-puncher. That land of the West has gone now, "gone, gone with lost Atlantis," gone to the isle of ghosts and of strange dead memories. It was a land of vast silent spaces, of lonely rivers, and of plains where the wild game stared at the passing horseman. It was a land of scattered ranches, of herds of long-horned cattle, and of reckless riders who unmoved looked in the eyes of life or of death. In that land we led a free and hardy life, with horse and with rifle. We worked under the scorching midsummer sun, when the wide plains shimmered and wavered in the heat; and we knew the freezing misery of riding night guard round the cattle in the late fall round-up. In the soft springtime the stars were glorious in our eyes each night before we fell asleep; and in the winter we rode through blinding blizzards, when the driven snow-dust burned our faces. There were monotonous days, as we guided the trail cattle or the beef herds, hour after hour, at the slowest of walks; and minutes or hours teeming with excitement as we stopped stampedes or swam the herds across rivers treacherous with quicksands or brimmed with running ice. We knew toil and hardship and hunger and thirst; and we saw men die violent deaths as they worked among the horses and cattle, or fought in evil feuds with one another; but we felt the beat of hardy life in our veins, and ours was the glory of work and the joy of living. . . .

I do not believe there ever was any life more attractive to a vigorous young fellow than life on a cattle-ranch in those days. It was a fine, healthy life, too; it taught a man self-reliance, hardihood, and the value of instant decision — in short, the virtues that ought to come from life in the open country. I enjoyed the life to the full.

An Autobiography

The charm of ranch life comes in its freedom and the vigorous open-air existence it forces a man to lead.

Hunting Trips of a Ranchman

My home-ranch stands on the river brink. From the low, long veranda, shaded by leafy cottonwoods, one looks across sand-bars and shallows to a strip of meadowland, behind which rises a line of sheer cliffs and grassy plateaus.

Reconstruction of Roosevelt's ranch house
in North Dakota's badlands.

This veranda is a pleasant place in the summer evenings
when a cool breeze stirs along the river and blows in the
faces of the tired men, who loll back in their rocking-chairs
(what true American does not enjoy a rocking-chair?),
book in hand — though they do not often read the books,
but rock gently to and fro, gazing sleepily out at the weird-
looking buttes opposite, until their sharp lines grow in-
distinct and purple in the afterglow of the sunset. The
story-high house of hewn logs is clean and neat, with many
rooms, so that one can be alone if one wishes to. The nights
in summer are cool and pleasant, and there are plenty of
bearskins and buffalo-robes, trophies of our own skill, with
which to bid defiance to the bitter cold of winter. In
summer-time, we are not much within doors, for we rise
before dawn and work hard enough to be willing to go to
bed soon after nightfall. The long winter evenings are
spent setting round the hearthstone, while the pine logs
roar and crackle, and the men play checkers or chess in the
firelight. The rifles stand in the corners of the room or rest
across the elk-antlers which jut out from over the fireplace.
From the deer-horns ranged along with walls and thrust
into the beams and rafters hang heavy overcoats of
wolfskin or coonskin, and otter-fur or beaver-fur caps
and gauntlets.

Hunting Trips of a Ranchman

Fireweed and Western hemlock on Washington's Olympic Peninsula.

*The rain-shrouded mountain chains of Oregon and
Washington are matted with mighty evergreen forests. . .*

Manifold are the shapes taken by the American wilderness. In the east, from the Atlantic coast to the Mississippi valley, lies a land of magnificent hardwood forest. In the endless variety and beauty, the trees cover the ground, save only where they have been cleared away by man, or where towards the west the expanse of the forest is broken by fertile prairies. Towards the north, this region of hardwood trees merges insensibly into the southern extension of the great subarctic forest; here the silver stems of birches gleam against the sombre background of coniferous evergreens. In the southeast again, by the hot, oozy coasts of the South Atlantic and the Gulf, the forest becomes semi-tropical; palms wave their feathery fronds, and the tepid swamps teem with reptile life. . . .

Beyond the plains rise the Rocky Mountains, their flanks covered with coniferous woods; but the trees are small, and do not ordinarily grow very close together. Towards the north the forest becomes denser, and the peaks higher; and glaciers creep down towards the valleys from the fields of everlasting snow. The brooks are brawling, trout-filled torrents; the swift rivers foam over rapid and cataract, on their way to one or the other of the two great oceans.

Southwest of the Rockies evil and terrible deserts stretch for leagues and leagues, mere waterless wastes of sandy plain and barren mountain, broken here and there by narrow strips of fertile ground. Rain rarely falls, and there are no clouds to dim the brazen sun. The rivers run in deep canyons, or are swallowed by the burning sand; the smaller watercourses are dry throughout the greater part of the year.

Beyond this desert region rise the sunny Sierras of California, with their flower-clad slopes and groves of giant trees; and north of them, along the coast, the rain-shrouded mountain chains of Oregon and Washington matted with the towering growth of the mighty evergreen forest.

The Wilderness Hunter

Ed Cooper

We heard a gang of wild geese . . .

Riding with a pack train, day in and day out, becomes both monotonous and irritating, unless one is upheld by the hope of a game-country ahead, or by the delight of exploration of the unknown. Yet when buoyed by such a hope, there is pleasure in taking a train across so beautiful and wild a country as that which lay on the threshold of our hunting grounds in the Shoshones. We went over mountain passes, with ranges of scalped peaks on either hand; we skirted the edges of lovely lakes, and of streams with boulder-strewn beds; we plunged into depths of sombre woodland, broken by wet prairies. It was a picturesque sight to see the loaded pack-train stringing across one of these high mountain meadows, the motley colored line of ponies winding round the marshy spots through the bright green grass, while beyond rose the dark line of frowning forest, with lofty peaks towering in the background. Some of the meadows were beautiful with many flowers — goldenrod, purple aster, bluebells, white immortelles, and here and there masses of blood-red Indian pinks. In the park country, on the edges of the evergreen forest, were groves of delicate quaking aspen, the trees often growing to quite a height; their tremulous leaves were already changing to bright green and yellow, occasionally with a reddish blush.

The Wilderness Hunter

Whoever has long roamed and hunted in the wilderness always cherishes with wistful pleasure the memory of some among the countless camps he has made. The camp by the margin of the clear, mountain-hemmed lake; the camp in the dark and melancholy forest, where the gusty wind booms through the tall pine tops; the camp under gnarled cottonwoods, on the bank of a shrunken river, in the midst of endless grassy prairies — of these, and many like them, each has had its own charm.

The Wilderness Hunter

One of the pleasantest times of camping out is the period immediately after supper, when the hunters lie in the blaze of the fire-light, talking over what they have done during the day and making their plans for the morrow. And how soundly a man who has worked hard sleeps in the open, none but he who has tried it knows.

Hunting Trips of a Ranchman

Above: Flock of Canada geese at
Quivera National Wildlife Refuge, Kansas.
Opposite: A climber tackles El Capitan
in Yosemite Valley, California.

In the spring when the thickets are green, the hermit thrushes sing sweetly in them; when it is moonlight, the voluble, cheery notes of the thrashers or brown thrushes can be heard all night long. One of our sweetest, loudest songsters is the meadow-lark; this I could hardly get used to at first, for it looks exactly like the Eastern meadow-lark, which utters nothing but a harsh disagreeable chatter. But the plains air seems to give it a voice, and it will perch on the top of a bush or tree and sing for hours in rich, bubbling tones. Out on the prairie there are several kinds of plains sparrows which sing very brightly, one of them hovering in the air all the time, like a bobolink. Sometimes, in the early morning, when corssing the open, grassy plateaus, I have heard the prince of them all, the Missouri skylark. The skylark sings on the wing, soaring overhead and mounting in spiral curves until it can hardly be seen, while its bright, tender strains never cease for a moment.

Hunting Trips of a Ranchman

One cool afternoon in the early fall, while sitting on the veranda of the ranch-house, we heard a long way off the *ha-ha-honk, ha-honk,* of a gang of wild geese; and shortly after they came in sight, in a V-shaped line, flying low and heavily toward the south, along the course of the stream. They went by within a hundred yards of the house, and we watched them for some minutes as they flew up the valley, for they were so low in the air that it seemed certain that they would soon alight; and alight they did when they were less than a mile past us.

Hunting Trips of a Ranchman

A toad beneath giant mushrooms. Roosevelt was interested in all forms of wildlife, from the large mammals to the small insects.

Of American big game the bison, almost always known as the buffalo, was the largest and most important to man. When the first white settlers landed in Virginia the bison ranged east of the Alleghenies almost to the seacoast, westward to the dry deserts lying beyond the Rocky Mountains, northward to the Great Slave Lake and southward to Chihuahua. It was a beast of the forests and mountains, in the Alleghenies no less than in the Rockies; but its true home was on the prairies and the high plains. Across these it roamed, hither and thither, in herds of enormous, of incredible magnitude; herds so large that they covered the waving grass land for hundreds of square leagues, and when on the march occupied days and days in passing a given point. But the seething myriads of shaggy-maned wild cattle, vanished with remarkable and melancholy rapidity before the inroads of the white hunters, and the steady march of the oncoming settlers. Now they are on the point of extinction. Two or three hundred are left in that great national game preserve, the Yellowstone Park; and it is said that others still remain in the wintry desolation of Athabasca. Elsewhere only a few individuals exist — probably considerably less than half a hundred all told — scattered in small parties in the wildest and most remote and inaccessible portions of the Rocky Mountains. A bison bull is the largest American animal. His huge bulk, his short, curved black horns, the shaggy mane clothing his great neck and shoulders, give him a look of ferocity which his conduct belies. Yet he is truly a grand and noble beast, and his loss from our prairies and forest is as keenly regretted by the lover of nature and of wildlife as by the hunter. . . .

The antelope, or prong-buck, was once found in abundance from the eastern edge of the great plains to the Pacific, but it has everywhere diminshed in numbers, and has been exterminated along the eastern and western borders of its former range. . . .

The cougar and wolf, once common throughout the United States, have now completely disappeared from all save the wildest regions.

The Wilderness Hunter

The call of the wapiti is one of the grandest and most beautiful sounds in nature. Especially is this the case when several rivals are answering one another, on some frosty moonlight night in the mountains. The wild melody rings from chasm to chasm under the giant pines, sustained and modulated, through bar after bar, filled with challenge and proud anger. It thrills the soul of the listening hunter.

The Wilderness Hunter

Ray Janusiak

An elk (wapiti) grazes in a meadow in Yellowstone National Park, Wyoming.

Essential to the park is the preservation of scenery for the people . . .

In the Grand Canyon, Arizona has a natural wonder which, so far as I know, is in kind absolutely unparalleled throughout the rest of the world. I want to ask you to do one thing in connection with it in your own interest and in the interest of the country — to keep this great wonder of nature as it is. I hope you will not have a building of any kind, not a summer cottage, a hotel, or anything else, to mar the wonderful grandeur, the sublimity, the great loneliness and beauty of the Canyon. You can not improve it. The ages have been at work on it, and man can only mar it.

Speech at Grand Canyon, 1903

I have thoroughly enjoyed having John Burroughs with me [touring Yellowstone National Park]. Porcupines and seemingly also skunks have diminished in the park during the last twelve years. Coyotes are numerous. Apparently there are no gray wolves. I have just found where a cougar killed a big bull elk. . . . The water ousel stays here all winter. I have heard it sing beautifully this time, and also the solitaire.

Letter to C. Hart Merriam, 1903

I cannot too often repeat that the essential feature in the present management of the Yellowstone Park, as in all similar places, is its essential democracy — it is the preservation of the scenery, of the forests, of the wilderness life and the wilderness game for the people as a whole, instead of leaving the enjoyment thereof to be confined to the very rich who can control private reserves.

Speech at Yellowstone, 1903

I trust I need not tell you, my dear sir, how happy were the days in the Yosemite I owed to you, and how greatly I appreciated them. I shall never forget our three camps; the first in the solemn temple of the great sequoias; the next in the snow storm among the silver firs near the brink of the cliff; and the third on the floor of the Yosemite, in the open valley fronting the stupendous rocky mass of El Capitan with the falls thundering in the distance on either hand.

Letter to John Muir, 1903

Lying out at night under those giant sequoias was like lying in a temple built by no hand of man, a temple grander than any human architect could by any possibility build, and I hope for the preservation of the groves of giant trees simply because it would be a shame to our civilization to let them disappear. They are monuments in themselves.

Speech at Sacramento, 1903

Opposite: A hiker pauses at Whitewater Falls in the southern Appalachians, North Carolina. *Below:* Middle Fork of the Feather River, northern California.

U. S. Forest Service

80

A giant redwood along California's northern coast. Udall believes that America is in a quiet conservation crisis and that we are faced with a diminishing quality environment and vanishing natural beauty. Fortunately, many Americans have awakened to the need of preserving what beauty is left. A good example is Redwood National Park, established in California in 1968, Udall's last year as Secretary of the Interior, after a decades-long struggle to protect these trees from outside interests.

STEWART L. UDALL

ᵛ America's Parklands at the Crossroads

At Cape Lookout on the magnificent outer banks of North Carolina, I watched a sea gull beat its lonely way against a sudden rainstorm that lashed the Atlantic shore. Leaning into the wind, the taste of the salt spray on my lips, I walked for miles along this isolated stretch of sand and dunes, soothed by the roar of crashing waves.

Only a few weeks before, President Johnson had signed legislation passed by the 89th Congress authorizing the establishment of this beautiful 58-mile barrier beach as the Cape Lookout National Seashore. Now, children of all generations would be assured of a place to watch sea gulls and sanderlings chase the waves — or see great flights of migratory birds take refuge in salt marshes along the Atlantic flyway — or build their world of tomorrow on the white sands of a timeless shore.

Who can trace the genesis of "the national park idea"? Many believe it was born in the year 1864 when President Lincoln signed the act transferring the beautiful Yosemite Valley and Mariposa Grove of Big Trees to the State of California ". . . for public use, resort and recreation." But the "idea" certainly gained its fullest recognition in the Act of 1872 establishing Yellowstone National Park — the first of its kind in the world. In this act, the Congress spelled out a new public land policy — that the scenic masterpieces of the public domain were to be dedicated and set apart in perpetuity — not for material gain or riches — but, rather, for the benefit and enjoyment of all the people "as a public park or pleasuring ground."

National Park Service, Williams

Stewart Udall (right), here enjoying spring along the C&O Canal in Maryland, is the author of several books, including *The National Parks of America* and *America's Natural Treasures,* from which the excerpts in this chapter have been taken, except where noted.

Breaking camp in the Sawtooth
Wilderness Area, Idaho.

U. S. Forest Service

Muir's personality combined the attitudes and insights of two pioneer U. S. naturalists, John James Audubon and Henry David Thoreau. On the basis of his experiences in California in the 1880's, Muir became an aggressive advocate of laws to set aside and preserve inviolate the scenic treasures of the country. Muir wrote crusading articles, harassed legislators, cajoled Presidents — and founded the Sierra Club. Largely as a result of his leadership, the Yellowstone example was magnified, and a string of superb new national parks — Yosemite, Mount Rainier, Crater Lake, Glacier and Mesa Verde — were created.

It was Muir who also exposed the principal flaw in the original national park concept. The final years of his life were dominated by a fight to prevent the building of a dam in the Hetch Hetchy valley within the newly established Yosemite park. He lost this battle, but the bitter controversy he aroused demonstrated that none of the parks were really preserved unless there were laws to prevent invasions by user groups. His fight also underscored the fact that each park needed a conservation-minded superintendent who would fight to protect his lands against all comers.

One of the men who came under Muir's influence was President Theodore Roosevelt. In 1903, they camped out together in Yosemite National Park and Muir expounded his conservation concepts far into the night. Roosevelt, a President who had a feeling for the outdoors matched by few other chief executives, proved to be an apt pupil. In 1906, when Congress passed a seemingly innocuous act giving Presidents the power to sign proclamations creating "national monuments . . . to preserve historic landmarks . . . and other objects of historic or scientific interests," TR had the action weapon he needed. In short order he proclaimed eighteen national monuments in various parts of the U.S., including four — Grand Canyon, Olympic, Lassen and Petrified Forest — which were so majestic Congress later made them national parks. This stroke-of-the-pen statesmanship set a pattern that enabled later Presidents to give park protection to millions of acres of scenic lands in the public domain.

Welcome to The Last Wilderness. Although other states may have patches of wilderness, only Alaska's is so primeval and untamed that you could wander for weeks without seeing another human being. It is the kind of wilderness that even people who know they will never see it are deeply satisfied that it still exists.

Mount St. Helens, a volcanic cone, in
Pinchot National Forest, Washington.

U.S. Forest Service

The spirit of the wolf
hangs over the land. Unseen,
his presence is felt . . .

Timber wolf, Alaska.

Ed Simpson

The Wilderness of Denali is not tamed. It is raw and primal, and a man feels very small in it. Almost anywhere off the one road he is truly alone — and sometimes a little afraid.

It is a vast land, which dwarfs normal scales. Sprawling river bars, peopled with the swarming specks that are the caribou, wind out of immensity at the foot of the hills. The wind across the tundra is clean, untainted by mankind.

The spirit of the wolf hangs over the land. Unseen, his presence is felt. He is the warden and unwitting benefactor of the caribou, the superb culmination of the biotic pyramid — and the personification of the wild.

Over all, the Alaska Range rises in a succession of brilliant ridges, cornices, peaks — each magnificent in its own right, but nearly lost in the greater picture. Higher they rise, leading the eye to the massive upsurge that is *The Mountain*. A full three vertical miles above the living tundra soars its peak.

Nothing lives on the mountain, but the mountain lives. Avalanches leap from its walls. Seracs crash; glaciers rumble and grind. Clouds swirl about its flanks, and a snow plume is torn by the wind from its uppermost crests. In the evening, the glare of the eternal ice softens, glows with the color of fireweed, then pales to ivory against the sky.

Whatever the season, the mountain, once seen, even if its persistent shroud of clouds allows only a momentary view, becomes an indelible recollection. The wildness of the park, once experienced, even if at some distance, leaves its mark on a man.

Warm breath freezes in the wet coldness of the dark morning, as the mountains await the sun's heat. From the east, the first rays of the coming day edge over the vast land forms, and one by one the dawn's fingers touch the great peaks, illuminating their snow with a pink, then orange, and finally white light. The mists on the upper peaks begin to break and slowly dissipate, and the full majesty of these mountains comes into full view. . . . Montana's Glacier National Park and the Grand Tetons of Wyoming have their glories, but the vast rock cathedrals of Washington's northern Cascades have a scope and grandeur all their own.

Autumn moonrise over Priest Lake,
Kaniksu National Forest, Idaho.

Scarlet Indian paintbrush in the
Cascades, southern Washington.

*The forces that shape
life cycles are evident
in the biting sting
of salt water spray . . .*

A vast expanse of sand and sea makes up Assateague Island National Seashore. Thirty-seven miles long and generally a mile to a mile and a half wide, this barrier island has many moods — from a quiet summer evening with the soothing wash of waves and the crying of terns the only sounds, to a winter storm raging over the sand, the surf thundering onto the sea.

The island was born of the sea and will die of the sea, as it is rapidly pushed toward the Delmarva Peninsula where three states (Delaware, Maryland and Virginia) share the Atlantic coastline.

A northeaster storm on Cape Hatteras has to be experienced to be believed. Raging wind blows sand with such force that it can be heard hitting a building, and the brushy plants bend away from the gusts, as if bowing to this master of violent nature. The seas crash their breakers into the shore, spray is hurled into the wind, and skies are ominously dark, the air filled with a cold, misty rain. A walk along the beach at this time is a walk in total loneliness, an experience unique to a place facing the sea such as this.

Marsh at Assateague National Seashore, Maryland, one of many parklands established near metropolitan areas in the 1960's and 1970's.

National Park Service

Pacific Ocean coastline, California.

Hours later, after the storm as passed, the beach takes on a different character. A warm breeze ruffles the drying sea oats and the setting sun plays with the clouds. A ghost crab scurries into the wet sand at your approach; scavenging shorebirds look for culinary delights at the edge of each dying breaker. Small sand dunes now exist where earlier there had been none, and others have disappeared.

The exhilarating aspects of winter storms on Cape Cod moved naturalist Henry David Thoreau to write that these periods were the best time to visit the area. Thoreau is credited with giving the name Great Beach to the seaside sands of the Cape. "A man can stand there and put all America behind him," he wrote. The elemental forces that shape life cycles are evident here in the biting sting of salt water spray borne in the teeth of a northeaster or in the offshore breeze of a quiet July afternoon.

Rooted strongly in sand dunes and silts, the cattails, marsh grass, bearberry, heath and pitch-pine woods stand against the rasping waters, collecting new sand from each windstorm. Glacial movement in the area resulted in an overlapping of northern and southern plant life growing on the Cape. Extensive geological evidence found in the accumulation of glacial drift makes the Cape a lodestone for geo-oceanographers.

Starfish at low tide, Cape Perpetua, Oregon.

89

The Great River, or Rio Grande, running a fairly straight southeast course, edging the United States and Mexico across the Chihuahua desert, suddenly bends around to its left, cuts to the north past the Chisos Mountains — for a total of 107 miles. And before it turns south again it puts a heart-shaped lower boundary on Big Bend National Park.

Here is the wilderness. Here is the unexplored. Here is the West (with a capital letter) in all of its desert and mountain and storybook wildness. . . .

This is a proud solitary stretch of country, harsh without bitterness, austere without anger and silent with a profound and brooding unfathomable mystery.

Even the suddenly green pockets of lush cottonwood-lined oases along the river's edge seem like gentle guests (rather than settlers) of the sweeping mesa and rolling mountain land that tolerate their being there with the preoccupied hospitality of a host who has great matters on his mind.

Cactus is not the only type of vegetation in Organ Pipe Cactus National Monument. If winter rains have been sufficient, spring may bring with it an array of desert colors — the bright red, showy flowers of the ocotillo; the greenish-yellow, nearly inconspicuous blossoms of the holacantha or crucifixion-thorn; and the pale yellow of the creosote bush. The brilliant red flowers of the desert honeysuckle attract many hummingbirds, and insects swarm over the drooping, pale yellow flower clusters of the mesquite. The leafless smokethorn or smoke tree from the California Microphyll Desert is covered in late spring with small, violet-to-indigo flowers, and in early summer the large white fragrant flowers of the night-blooming cereus open at dusk. The paloverde, with its dense mantle of yellow blossoms, forms a ribbon of gold over the land for many spring months.

The wind blows gently down this vast wound in the earth, rippling the surface of its creative force, the river, and carrying occasional small puffs of red dust from the awesome walls. The breeze wanes and the eerie silence fans out in four directions, held captive within the impenetrable fortress nature spent nine million years to create.

The Grand Canyon is true to its name, yet a mere, momentary glance prods the beholder's mind, searching for a word more expressive than "Grand". . . .

Opposite: Golden poppies in desert, Tonto National Forest, central Arizona.
Below: Prickly-pear cactus, Badlands National Monument, South Dakota.

National Park Service

This is a land where rock is master. It is everywhere in every form and shape imaginable . . .

This is a land where rock is master. It is everywhere in every form and shape imaginable, as if other objects had somehow been changed into it. You can see the sheer, vertical walls of a building, the swirls of a giant vat of rippled ice cream, the spires of a grand European cathedral, a Roman viaduct's arches, a waterfall's cascades, the pyramids of Egypt, the towers and columns of a Spanish castle — all are rock.

The Colorado Plateau contains the most colorful, varied, sculptured land on the face of the earth, and Arches is one of its masterpieces. In this 137-square-mile national park in southeastern Utah, sedimentary rock, formed in lakes and floods before the memory of man, has been shaped gloriously by the carving tools of wind-blown sand, frost and moisture. The result is a superb display of eroded formations that together form a collection of stone arches, windows, spires and pinnacles unequalled in this country.

Heat waves shimmer in the scorching sun as it beats down upon the flats and crags of this barren valley situated between severe mountain ridges rising from a distant desert. It is a heartless master, this valley, unchanged by the softening touch of time. Man's efforts to tame this wilderness seem puny, dwarfed by heaps of lava, burst stone and many-hued clays cast up from beneath the earth's crust in some ancient cataclysm.

Indians who once dwelled in nearby mountains and attempted to harvest a little food from the sparse vegetation called the valley *tomesha*, meaning "red earth," because it yielded a fire-colored clay that warriors used to produce warpaint for their bodies. Sourdough mountain men claimed the Indian word meant "ground afire." But the name that finally attached itself unshakeably to this harsh valley is Death Valley.

The name is inappropriate, for this is a land of light, color and considerable beauty. Each shift of light, shadow or perspective casts a different spell because of the infinite variations of color, form and texture.

Park Avenue, a formation of rocks in Arches National Park, Utah.

Nebraska Game and Parks Commission

Yellow prairie coneflowers, Nebraska.

The death of these Indiana dunes — and that hushed wood lot or clean spring you mourn today in your community — has a fitting epitaph in the words of President Kennedy as he urged creation of a Land Conservation Fund: "In conserving our national outdoor areas, opportunities delayed generally mean opportunities lost."

The list of opportunities delayed and opportunities lost grows each year.

A proposal to create a Prairie National Park in Kansas was derided by some who maintained that no public action was necessary, so vast were the remaining prairie lands. A few weeks later a developer announced plans to build three hundred homes, a golf course and an airport on a portion of the proposed site. . . .

Virtually every community can compile its own list of opportunities lost as freeways, industrial plants and subdivisions march into our open spaces at the rate of a million acres a year, destroying the flavor of wilderness, exchanging the forest for the prefab, the fresh air for the diesel's exhalations.

We will go on compiling these post-mortems until we as a nation embrace the realization that opportunities for open space acquisition are lost not because public appreciation and support of their cause is lacking, but in many cases simply because no funds, either private or public, have been available for their purchase.

And unless we provide the Federal Government and the states with new sources of revenue for open space land acquisition, there will be more and more dunes, woodlands and clear streams listed by succeeding generations as "opportunities lost."

"The Outdoors Is No Longer Free," 1963

In the 1960's, during my eight years as Secretary of the Interior, new problems and new ecological insights caused us to recognize the impact of activities which were to that time considered "outside" the parks. . . When evidence accumulated that the widespread use of DDT and other hard pesticides was destroying the reproductive capacities of eagles, ospreys and other birds, we realized we had to take sides with Rachel Carson in the fight against long-lived poisons. And when small streams in the urbanized areas of Yellowstone and Yosemite were polluted, we realized that a process of "deurbanizing" these areas had to begin. . . .

The national parks play an important role in our national life. They give refreshing outdoor experiences to millions of Americans; they serve as wilderness laboratories for scientists and they are outdoor classrooms for Americans of all ages who want to understand

Rocky Mountain bighorn sheep
on the National Bison Range, Montana.

the natural world. Most important, they have helped make
the wilderness ethic — with its inherent skepticism of
mechanized "progress" — part of our national creed.

But these contributions notwithstanding, the Yellowstone centenary finds our parklands in serious trouble today. Ecologists have warned that no park, however remote,
is an island which can wholly escape the impacts of modern
man and his machines. Rivers and winds and ocean tides
carry pollutants and poisons everywhere. In the long run
even these protected enclaves will be slowly impaired unless the planetary environmental crisis is resolved.

In the long run (and park planning is meaningless unless it adopts the long haul perspective), there is reason to
fear that the parks will succumb slowly to the pressures of
growth — unless restraint becomes a new national im-
perative. If our demand for raw materials and other natural
resources doubles four or five times by the year 2072, I
believe it is certain that events will force us to exploit the
petroleum and mineral deposits beneath our national
parks. If the current statistical projections are fulfilled and
the nation's population reaches, say, five hundred million
in the next one hundred years, it is unlikely that the parks
as we know them today can survive except as trampled
remnants of the original America.

Backpacking in Yosemite National Park, California.